THIS WAS NOT THE PLAN

This Was Not the Plan

Ujjaval Bothra

First Printing, 2026

Contents

Credit Note

- Book Curation and Execution: **Ms. Pratiksha Kankaria**
- Frameworks and Learning Direction: **Mr. Sachin Talwar**

Acknowledgement

No Kahani is ever created alone. This book, this journey, and every celebration I have been part of exist because of the people who walked beside me through every challenge and every moment of growth.

To my **family**, for trusting my path even when it made no sense. Your belief carried me through the hardest phases, and your love shaped the person behind this book.

Gratitude to my **parents** for their endless support, my brothers for always being there, and every Kahani ka kirdaar—our team, vendors, clients and venues — who believed in this journey and made it possible.

To my **team at Kahani**, you are the heartbeat of everything we create. Each one of you brings a piece of your soul into our work. Your sincerity, calmness and commitment transform ideas into memories. This book belongs to you as much as it belongs to me.

To the **families, couples, corporates** and **communities** who trusted us with their most important moments. Thank you for giving me the honour of stepping into your lives. Every project, every hug and every smile taught me something new.

And finally, to the **young planners** and **dreamers** in this industry. This book is my small contribution to your growth. May you create celebrations that touch hearts and stories that live forever.

Love & Gratitude
Ujjaval Bothra

Preface

Celebrations have always fascinated me. Not because of the decor or the glamour or the scale, but because of the emotions that move quietly beneath the surface. Over the past twelve years, I have seen families cry with joy, corporate leaders breathe in relief, couples laugh without fear, and entire gatherings transform into memories that last a lifetime. Somewhere along this journey, I realised something profound. A celebration is not just an event. It is a story. A story of people, of decisions, of emotions, of trust and of moments that will never happen again.

This book was born from that realisation. The world sees the beauty of a celebration, but not its backbone. They see the lights, not the planning. They see the decor, not the intention. They see the performers, not the coordination. They see the moment, not the journey. Through this book, I want to open the door to that hidden world. I want you to see how calmness, structure, empathy and creativity come together to create magic. Magic that feels effortless on the outside because there is so much depth on the inside.

If this book helps even one family celebrate with more sukoon, one host feel more confident, or one young planner discover purpose in this industry, then the Kahani has done its job.

Foreword

Some books teach you skills. Some books share experiences. And then some books make you pause and reflect on what it really takes to hold things together when life doesn't go as planned.

This Was Not the Plan is one such book.

I have known the author not just as a founder, a leader, or a storyteller but as my younger brother. I've seen his journey from close quarters, often quietly, often from the background. While his world has always been fast, loud, emotional, and full of risk, mine has been steadier, more measured. Perhaps that is why this book moved me the way it did.

This is not a book about events.
It is a book about people.

About the weight that comes with responsibility.
About decisions taken under pressure.
About nights when nothing goes right, yet you still show up the next morning.
About holding calm when chaos refuses to settle.

What stands out most is the honesty. The stories here don't romanticise perfection. They acknowledge fear, doubt, anxiety, and the quiet moments of exhaustion that no one applauds. They remind us that celebrations don't succeed because everything goes according to plan; they succeed. After all, someone chooses to stay steady when the plan falls apart.

At its heart, this book is about execution guided by emotion.

About doing the work with care.

About understanding that behind every smooth celebration is a team carrying invisible pressure with visible grace.

Reading these pages, you can sense the pulse of the people behind the scenes, the teamwork, the trust, the unspoken understanding. You can feel how chaos slowly turns into clarity, and how experience is built not in grand moments, but in small, difficult ones that demand patience and courage.

This book is also about becoming.

Becoming stronger without becoming harder.

Becoming braver without losing sensitivity.

Becoming a leader who listens, feels, and still delivers.

For me, this book is not just a reflection of one person's journey. It is a reminder that growth doesn't always look dramatic. Sometimes, it looks like consistency. Sometimes, it looks like standing your ground. And sometimes, it looks like continuing even when this was not the plan.

If you are reading this book, I hope you find pieces of your own journey within it. I hope it reminds you that it's okay when plans fail because effort, intention, and heart still matter.

And most of all, I hope it reminds you that behind every celebration, every milestone, and every moment that works there is always a Kahani worth acknowledging.

Mohit Bothra
Elder Brother

Why This Book

Celebrations look simple from the outside. A beautiful mandap, a perfectly timed entry, a corporate gala where everything appears to flow smoothly. But behind every perfect moment lies a world that people rarely understand. A world filled with decisions, emotions and tiny details that can change the entire experience.

Most hosts, couples and even young planners believe events are about decoration and execution. But the truth is deeper. Great celebrations are born from emotional intelligence, structured planning and a deep sense of responsibility. They are built on sukoon, not stress. On clarity, not chaos. On intention, not impulse.

I wrote this book because our industry needs more understanding. Families deserve to know what truly creates peace during a wedding. Corporates deserve to understand what elevates their events. And planners deserve a window into the mindset and systems that transform work into art.

This book exists to reveal the Kahani behind the moments that feel magical.

Know Your Author

Ujjaval Bothra is the founder of Kahani, a company that has redefined weddings, corporate events and curated celebrations through its unique blend of emotion, creativity and structured execution. His journey did not begin with a grand plan. It began with life nudging him toward spaces where people, stories and experiences mattered more than titles. After spending years in the corporate world observing how relationships shape outcomes, he realised he wanted to build something more human. Something that touched hearts. Something that created sukoon. That instinct slowly grew into Kahani.

His early journey was filled with mistakes, misalignment and difficult phases that forced him to pause and reinvent himself. He learned that calmness is non-negotiable, accountability begins at the top, and a business grows only when the person leading it grows first. With renewed clarity and discipline, he rebuilt Kahani into a purpose-driven team known for apnapan, thoughtful hospitality and seamless storytelling.

Today, after curating more than one thousand events across India, Ujjaval stands as a leader who believes celebrations are not projects but emotions. He has trained and inspired many young planners, created meaningful impact through community initiatives and shaped an approach where every celebration becomes a Kahani worth remembering.

Introduction

Every perfect celebration tells a story. A story that guests may never know, but they always feel. Over the years, as I worked on weddings, corporate events and social gatherings across India, I realised that every celebration has two worlds. The world that people see, and the world that actually creates the moment.

The seen world is filled with beauty. Lights are glowing softly. Music rises at the right moment. Families hugging. Celebrities performing. Guests laughing. Executives networking. Photographers capture a memory that may never repeat.

But the unseen world is where the real Kahani unfolds. A world where decisions are made with care, vendors are coordinated with precision, emotions are understood with sensitivity and countless people work silently to ensure everything feels effortless. It is a world where chaos is turned into calm and planning is turned into poetry.

This book is my attempt to bring those two worlds together for you. It is a collection of lessons, stories, and principles that I have learned through thousands of interactions, successes, challenges and moments that shaped me. Whether you are a couple getting married, a family hosting a milestone celebration, a corporate planning an important event or an aspiring planner looking for direction, this book will help you understand what really makes celebrations perfect. Because behind every moment you cherish, there is always a Kahani. **Kahaniyon se pyaar hai, Kahaniyon ka Vyapaar hai!**

1

What Makes a Wedding or Event Truly Stress Free

"A stress-free celebration is not one without problems. It is one where problems dissolve before they reach you."

A stress-free celebration is often misunderstood as an event where nothing goes wrong. In reality, nothing ever goes exactly as planned. Timelines shift, people arrive late, emotions rise unexpectedly, and circumstances change without warning. What truly defines a stress-free wedding or event is not the absence of challenges, but the presence of a system and mindset that ensures those challenges never burden the people who are meant to enjoy the moment.

Every family, every host and every corporate leader carries the same silent wish during an important event. They want the freedom to be present. The freedom to smile without constantly checking the clock. The freedom to engage in conversations without worrying about what is happening backstage. They want to live the moment rather than manage it. That freedom only comes when responsibility rests in the right hands. Jab zimmedari kisi sahi haath mein hoti hai, sukoon apne aap aa jaata hai, bina kisi conscious effort ke.

In weddings, stress is deeply emotional. Parents carry years of dreams, expectations and unspoken pressure to create something memorable for their children. The couple wants to experience every ritual without distraction, to laugh freely, to cry without interruption, and to remember the day as a blur of joy rather than a series of instructions. Guests arrive with their own expectations of comfort, hospitality and experience. Every emotion adds a layer of pressure. In corporate events, the stress takes a different shape but carries equal weight. Brand image, professional credibility, timelines and guest perception are all at stake. One visible misstep can overshadow months of preparation.

Yet in both worlds, the root cause of stress remains the same. Too many moving parts without a single point of ownership.

This is where the role of a capable planning team becomes transformative. A strong team does not merely coordinate vendors or execute tasks; it also fosters collaboration and drives innovation. They take ownership of the entire experience. From timelines and flow to hospitality, technical precision and emotional moments, they become the invisible anchor holding everything together. When ownership is clear, confusion reduces automatically. When confusion reduces, stress dissolves.

Consider a situation that happens far more often than people realise. A wedding baraat gets delayed or a keynote speaker arrives late due to travel issues. On the surface, it seems manageable. But beneath it, panic begins to build. Catering schedules shift. Decor lighting cues get disturbed. Guests start asking questions. Family members begin calling each other. In poorly managed events, this panic spreads quickly and becomes visible. In well-managed events, it dissolves silently. Timelines are adjusted. Teams are informed calmly. Alternate engagement is created for guests. The host remains largely unaware of the turbulence because someone else is absorbing it. Yeh wahi pal hota hai jahan planning ki asli taqat samajh aati hai.

Hospitality plays an equally important role in creating stress-free experiences. When guests are guided gently, elderly family members are assisted without being asked and logistical needs are anticipated in advance, the environment immediately feels lighter. These are not grand gestures. They are thoughtful details that prevent stress before it forms. A calm welcome, clear directions and warm human interaction reduce anxiety more effectively than any decoration ever could.

A stress-free event is never built on perfection. Perfection is fragile and breaks under pressure. Stress-free celebrations are built on trust. Trust that someone is watching the details. Trust that emotions are being handled with sensitivity. Trust that decisions are being made with clarity rather than panic. When that trust exists, families relax, couples enjoy their moments, and corporate hosts focus on their purpose instead of logistics.

At its core, a stress-free celebration is the result of one simple truth. When the right people take responsibility, the event stops feeling like a task and starts becoming a memory. And when memories are created with ease and warmth, that is when a celebration truly fulfils its purpose.

Action Points

- Clarity instantly reduces stress, bringing calmness and confidence.
- Shift focus from "everything must be perfect" to "everyone should feel comfortable."
- Build trust by delegating responsibilities to capable professionals or team members.
- Prioritise flow and timing over unnecessary detailing.

2

How Great Planners Turn Chaos Into Calm

"Calmness is the quiet confidence that everything will fall into place."

Every celebration, regardless of its scale or intent, carries an element of chaos. Weddings are filled with emotional highs, unpredictable timings and energetic crowds. Corporate events carry pressure, precision and fast-paced execution. Social gatherings sit somewhere in between. Chaos is not a sign of failure. It is a natural part of any event that brings people together. The difference lies in how that chaos is handled.

Great planners do not fear chaos. They expect it. They prepare for it. They understand that chaos is not something to eliminate but something to shape. They transform confusion into clarity and noise into harmony. Unki shanti poore event ka mood set kar deti hai.

Calmness is not accidental. It is built through preparation, structure and experience. When a planner has mapped out timelines, rehearsed cues, defined roles and prepared backups, they naturally operate with confidence. Calm planners anchor the entire environment. Teams listen better. Vendors cooperate more willingly. Families feel protected. Corporate clients feel assured. Calmness becomes contagious.

Imagine a wedding varmala about to begin or a product launch moment seconds away from execution. Suddenly, the sound system stops functioning. An inexperienced team panics. Voices rise. Blame circulates. Anxiety becomes visible. A seasoned team reacts differently. Backup systems are activated. Cues are adjusted. The moment continues without interruption. Guests never realise anything went wrong. Yeh hi asli kala hai. Managing chaos without letting chaos show.

Weather offers another common challenge. Outdoor weddings and events are constantly at the mercy of nature. A sudden wind, unexpected rain, or temperature change can disrupt carefully planned setups. A calm planning team responds with composure. Elements are shifted indoors. Manpower is reassigned. Guests are guided smoothly. The event adapts without losing dignity. Calm planners think in solutions, not problems.

Corporate events bring their own versions of chaos. Last-minute speaker changes, seating reshuffles, technical delays and VIP movements can create pressure. A composed team manages these situations quietly. They protect the pace and professionalism of the event while absorbing stress internally. The audience experiences confidence. The client experiences trust.

The true difference between chaos and calm is leadership. When the planner remains collected, the entire team mirrors that behaviour. Jab lead shant hota hai, team ko lagta hai sab control mein hai. That confidence flows outward and shapes the guest experience.

Calmness is not the absence of challenges. It is the presence of mastery. It is the ability to stand steady while everything moves around you. Great planners understand this deeply. They do not chase control. They create stability. And in doing so, they transform chaos into calm, moment after moment.

Action Points

- Prepare detailed plans, but rehearse adaptability more than rigidity.
- Communicate clearly with every stakeholder-teams, vendors, and family members.
- Always build backups for timelines, speakers, weather, and logistics.
- Lead calmly; the team mirrors the leader's emotional state.
- Solve problems quietly so guests never experience disruption.

3

The Secret Behind Effortless Celebrations

"Effortlessness is the outcome of preparation done quietly and consistently."

Effortless celebrations often look like magic to those experiencing them. Moments unfold smoothly, transitions feel natural, and everything seems to happen at just the right time. Guests walk away saying that the event felt easy, light and enjoyable. What they rarely realise is that effortlessness is never accidental. It is the visible result of invisible work done with patience, discipline and intention.

Every effortless wedding or event is built on deep preparation. What appears smooth on the surface is supported by layers of planning beneath it. Timelines are not just created but tested. Movements are not just imagined but rehearsed. Roles are not just assigned but clearly understood. When preparation is done thoroughly, execution feels gentle. Jab mehnat andar hoti hai, toh bahar aasaani dikhti hai.

Effortless events follow a simple yet powerful philosophy. Think ahead. Prepare deeply. Remove friction early. Anticipate needs before they are voiced. This approach separates ordinary planning from thoughtful planning. It allows the celebration to flow naturally without visible effort. When planners ask the right questions early, problems do not arise later. When systems are clear, confusion has no space to grow.

Consider a reception entry that feels cinematic. The lighting changes at the perfect moment, the music blends seamlessly with the ambience, and the couple walks in feeling confident and present. To a guest, this feels spontaneous. In reality, it comes from multiple rehearsals, technical checks and precise coordination between sound, light and movement. Similarly, in a corporate event, when a brand video plays exactly on cue, and the speaker walks on stage without delay, the moment feels powerful because it has been prepared repeatedly. None of this is a coincidence.

Guest experience is another space where effortlessness is deeply felt. When guests arrive and find their rooms ready, their luggage handled, and directions clearly communicated, they feel cared for. When corporate attendees experience smooth registration, comfortable seating and guided movement, they feel respected. Behind this ease lies coordination between hospitality, logistics and operations teams. Parde ke peeche bahut saare log shant tareeke se kaam karte hain, isliye saamne sab kuch smooth lagta hai.

Effortlessness is also built on systems. Clear timelines ensure that teams know what happens when. Defined responsibilities ensure that no task is assumed or forgotten. Backup plans ensure that unexpected situations do not disrupt the flow. These systems may never be noticed by guests, but they shape the entire experience.

Empathy plays an equally important role. When planners understand how a guest might feel while waiting, how a family member might feel during a ritual or how a speaker might feel before stepping on stage, they prepare accordingly. Effortlessness comes not only from structure but from sensitivity.

An effortless celebration is never about luck. It is intentional care disguised as ease. It is the result of people who plan quietly, execute thoughtfully and allow the moment to shine without interference. That is the true secret behind celebrations that feel magical.

Action Points

- Prepare more than what is visible; effortlessness is built at backstage.
- Anticipate needs before they arise-guest comfort, movement, and transitions.
- Rehearse critical moments to eliminate last-minute confusion.
- Build systems that allow people to perform without constant supervision.
- Remember: if it feels smooth, it's because someone planned deeply.

4

What Top Hosts Do Differently While Planning

"The best results come to those who prepare thoughtfully, not hurriedly."

Top families and experienced hosts approach celebrations differently. They do not see events as tasks to be completed, but as journeys to be experienced. Whether it is a destination wedding, a milestone anniversary or a high-profile corporate gathering, the hosts who achieve the most meaningful outcomes share a common mindset. Yeh log planning ko race ki tarah nahi, ek journey ki tarah dekhte hain.

The first difference lies in clarity of purpose. Before discussing decor, artists or scale, they take time to understand what they want the celebration to feel like. Families decide whether they want intimacy, grandeur or emotional depth. Corporate hosts define what they want their audience to remember and carry forward. Once the purpose is clear, decisions become simpler. Decor, hospitality, flow and communication naturally align with the intent.

Another key difference is timing. Top hosts begin planning early. They understand that rushing leads to compromises, while preparation creates space for better decisions. Early planning allows time for discussions, revisions and alignment. It also reduces last-minute pressure, which is one of the biggest contributors to stress. Jab time saath hota hai, toh planning bhi saath deti hai.

Choosing the right partners early is equally important. Experienced hosts involve planners who understand both emotion and execution. They value guidance and are open to suggestions. They communicate expectations honestly and allow professionals to translate those expectations into experiences. Jab sahi log shuru se saath hote hain, result naturally strong hota hai.

Trust is another defining trait. Top families and hosts trust the teams they hire. They do not micromanage every detail or second-guess every decision. Instead, they stay informed while allowing experts to execute. This trust reduces friction and enables creativity. When teams feel trusted, they take ownership. When ownership increases, quality improves.

Thoughtful hosts also prioritise guest experience. They think beyond how things will look and focus on how people will feel. For weddings, this means considering guest movement, comfort and emotional engagement. For corporate events, it means designing content flow, interaction and ease. They understand that celebrations are remembered through feelings, not visuals alone.

Finally, top hosts remain open and calm throughout the process. They accept that small changes may occur. They respond to challenges with flexibility rather than panic. They stay emotionally connected without becoming overwhelmed. Inka approach balanced hota hai. Emotional bhi aur practical bhi.

The difference between an average event and a remarkable one is rarely budget. It is a mindset. Hosts who lead with clarity, trust and intention create celebrations that feel meaningful, organised and deeply satisfying. And those celebrations leave a lasting impression on everyone involved.

Action Points

- Define the purpose of the celebration before planning anything else.
- Choose partners and planners based on trust, not just cost.
- Focus on how guests will *feel*, not just what they will *see*.
- Stay emotionally involved but operationally detached, let professionals execute.

5

How to Make Event Feel Personal & Unforgettable

"Personalisation is not about decoration. It is about emotion."

Every celebration that stays in memory does so for one simple reason. It makes people feel something. Long after the lights are switched off and the music fades, guests remember how they felt while being there. Personalisation is not about adding more elements to an event. It is about revealing meaning through thoughtful choices. Jab event mein kahani ghulti hai, tabhi woh yaadon mein bas jaata hai.

In weddings, personalisation begins with understanding the couple's journey. Their personalities, their shared memories, their families and the values they carry together. When planners take the time to listen deeply, small details begin to emerge naturally. A welcome note that reflects a shared inside joke, a playlist that mirrors the couple's story, or a decor element inspired by their roots can quietly transform a space. These gestures do not need to be grand. They need to be honest. Authenticity creates connection, and connection creates memory.

Corporate events may appear more structured, but personalisation plays an equally powerful role. Brands are not just logos or taglines. They are stories of people, growth and purpose. When an event reflects the brand's journey through thoughtful installations, curated content or meaningful stage moments, guests feel aligned with the intent. A founder's brief message, a timeline of milestones or a subtle visual narrative can turn a formal gathering into an engaging experience. When people feel connected to the purpose, they remember the event long after it ends.

Hospitality is one of the most overlooked yet impactful forms of personalisation. When guests receive a warm welcome that feels intentional, when VIPs are offered amenities that suit their preferences, or when elderly guests are guided gently, they feel seen. A small gesture of empathy often carries more weight than elaborate decor. Chhoti chhoti cheezein dil ko choo jaati hain, aur wahi cheezein event ko yaadgaar banaati hain.

Storytelling is another powerful layer of personalisation. Sharing a short journey film at a wedding, including a reflective note during a corporate milestone, or creating an installation that visually represents values adds depth. Stories anchor emotion. They give people context. When guests understand the story, they engage with the celebration on a deeper level.

True personalisation is subtle. It does not shout for attention. It reveals itself gently through details that feel thoughtful rather than forced. When an event reflects the people behind it, the celebration becomes more than an occasion. It becomes an experience that feels intimate, intentional and unforgettable.

Action Points

- Identify emotional anchors like stories, memories, values and that matter to the host.
- Personalise through meaning, not excess spending.
- Use storytelling to connect guests emotionally to the celebration.
- Add thoughtful details in hospitality, communication, and welcome moments.
- Keep experiences authentic; sincerity is more powerful than spectacle.

6

What Creates Guest Happiness at Scale

"Happy guests create the environment where memories grow."

Guest happiness is one of the most important measures of a successful celebration, yet it is often underestimated. Whether it is a wedding with thousands of attendees or a corporate summit hosting hundreds of professionals, the overall experience is shaped by how guests feel throughout the event. When guests feel cared for, their comfort spreads positivity across the entire space. Mehmaan khush toh mahol khush.

Clarity forms the foundation of guest happiness. Guests want to know where to go, what to expect and how to navigate the event. Clear signage, informed team members and smooth entry experiences set the tone immediately. Confusion creates anxiety, while clarity builds comfort. When guests feel oriented, they relax and begin to enjoy the celebration.

Hospitality plays a defining role, especially in weddings. A warm greeting, a friendly face guiding elderly family members, and well-managed check-ins signal respect. These gestures make guests feel valued. People may forget elaborate decor, but they always remember how they were treated. Ek pyaari si smile aur thoda sa dhyaan, guest experience ko next level pe le jaata hai.

Food and refreshment are equally significant. Timely service, thoughtful menu planning and attention to dietary needs enhance comfort. In corporate events, well-planned breaks, accessible water stations and comfortable seating keep energy levels balanced. Guests may not discuss the setup in detail, but they will talk about how smoothly everything flowed.

Logistics influence happiness more than most hosts realise. Smooth transportation, punctual shuttles and guided movement prevent frustration. When guests move easily from one space to another, the celebration feels organised and considerate. Movement should feel intuitive rather than forced.

Emotional hospitality adds the final layer. A small moment of assistance, a thoughtful note for VIPs, or a gentle escort for elderly guests can shift the entire experience. These actions communicate care. When guests sense that their comfort matters, they engage more openly with the celebration.

Guest happiness is not managed by a single department. It is a culture that runs through the entire team. When teams operate with empathy and awareness, large gatherings feel personal and welcoming. And when guests leave feeling content and cared for, the celebration achieves its true purpose.

Action Points

- Map the guest journey from arrival to departure.
- Ensure clarity at every touchpoint-signage, assistance, seating, and movement.
- Train teams to respond with warmth, not just efficiency.

- Remove friction points that cause confusion or waiting.
- Measure success by guest comfort, not applause.

7

Power of Thoughtful Design in Any Celebration

"Design is not decoration. Design is how an event feels."

Design is often the first thing people notice and the last thing they truly remember. Long after guests forget the exact arrangement of flowers or the placement of lights, they remember the feeling a space gave them. Thoughtful design has the power to shape emotion before a single word is spoken. Whether it is a wedding mandap, a sangeet stage, a conference hall or a product launch setup, design quietly sets the tone for everything that follows.

At its core, thoughtful design begins with intention. Before colours are chosen or structures are built, the most important question is asked. What should the guest feel when they enter this space? Comfort, excitement, warmth, elegance, inspiration. Once that emotion is defined, every design decision becomes clearer. Colours, textures, lighting and layout begin to align naturally with the feeling the host wants to create. Jab design soch se shuru hota hai, tabhi woh dil tak pahunchta hai.

In weddings, thoughtful design often reflects roots, values and personal stories. A mandap inspired by a family's heritage, a reception stage that mirrors the couple's personality or a subtle motif that repeats across spaces can create emotional continuity. These elements do not need to be loud. When they are meaningful, they speak quietly yet powerfully. Guests may not consciously analyse these details, but they feel the harmony they create.

In corporate events, design plays a different but equally critical role. It communicates brand identity and intent. A clean stage design signals professionalism. A dynamic installation encourages interaction. Breakout spaces designed for comfort invite conversation. When design aligns with brand values, the event feels intentional rather than ornamental. Guests instinctively understand what the brand stands for without being told.

Lighting is one of the most underestimated elements of thoughtful design. The right lighting can soften a space, energise a crowd or focus attention at the right moment. Warm lighting creates intimacy. Dramatic lighting builds excitement. Clean lighting establishes clarity. Lighting does not merely illuminate objects. It shapes mood. It guides attention. It supports storytelling.

Flow is another essential component of design. How guests move through a space affects how they experience it. When entry points are intuitive, seating is comfortable, and pathways are clear, the event feels effortless. When guests are unsure where to go, even the most beautiful setup loses its charm. Thoughtful design respects movement and human behaviour.

True design is never about excess. It is about coherence. When design respects emotion, culture and purpose, it elevates the celebration into an experience. It allows the space to speak before anyone else does. And when a space feels right, people relax into it naturally. That is the quiet power of thoughtful design.

Action Points

- Design with purpose, not trends.
- Align decor, lighting, music, and space with the emotion you want to evoke.
- Avoid visual overload; simplicity often creates stronger impact.
- Ensure functionality supports beauty and design must serve flow.
- Let design tell a story, not just decorate a space.

8

What Brings Emotion and Execution Together

"Emotion creates meaning. Execution creates trust."

The most memorable celebrations are those where emotion and execution move in harmony. Weddings are driven by emotion. Corporate events are driven by structure. Social gatherings sit at the intersection of both. The real magic appears when feeling and system support each other rather than compete. Jab dil aur dimaag ek saath kaam karte hain, tabhi celebration truly unforgettable banti hai.

Emotion without execution often leads to chaos. Good intentions get lost in confusion. Moments feel rushed. Experiences feel incomplete. On the other hand, execution without emotion feels mechanical. Everything happens on time, but nothing touches the heart. When both elements come together, celebrations feel both smooth and meaningful.

In weddings, emotions run deep and often unpredictably. Families experience joy, nostalgia, nervousness and pride all at once. Couples move between excitement and overwhelm. A team that understands these emotional layers works differently. They give families space during rituals. They communicate gently. They remain attentive without being intrusive. Emotion becomes part of planning rather than an obstacle to it.

In corporate events, execution takes centre stage. Timelines matter. Transitions must be precise. Brand representation must remain consistent. Yet emotion still plays a role. How guests are welcomed, how speakers are guided, how achievements are acknowledged. Emotion gives execution character. It transforms a functional event into an engaging experience.

Execution provides the structure that allows emotion to flow freely. It ensures that vendors arrive on time, stages are ready, hospitality runs smoothly, and technical cues align perfectly. When execution is strong, emotional moments are not interrupted by logistical distractions. Families feel secure. Hosts feel confident. Guests remain engaged.

The bridge between emotion and execution is empathy backed by preparation. When teams anticipate emotional needs and support them with strong systems, celebrations find their rhythm. Moments unfold naturally because the groundwork has already been laid.

Emotion touches the heart. Execution builds trust. Together, they create experiences that last beyond the event itself. This balance is not accidental. It is cultivated through awareness, discipline and care. And when achieved, it becomes the defining signature of truly exceptional celebrations.

Action Points

- Balance emotional sensitivity with operational discipline.
- Train teams to understand people, not just processes.

- Create systems that allow emotional moments to unfold without disruption.
- Protect the host from decision fatigue on the event day.
- Remember: execution is successful when emotions are undisturbed.

9

Why Some Events Feel Seamless From Start to End

"A seamless event is a story without breaks."

Some celebrations feel like they unfold in one gentle breath. From the moment guests arrive to the moment they leave, everything seems connected, calm and thoughtfully paced. Nothing feels rushed. Nothing feels abrupt. There is a rhythm to the experience that allows people to relax and simply be present. This seamlessness is not accidental. It is carefully designed long before the event begins.

Seamless celebrations begin with integration. Every element, whether decor, hospitality, sound, light or logistics, works in alignment rather than isolation. When teams communicate clearly and understand how their roles connect with one another, gaps disappear. Guests may never notice this alignment consciously, but they feel it deeply. Jab sab cheezein ek saath chalti hain, event khud ba khud behne lagta hai.

Flow is a critical element of seamlessness. A well-designed flow ensures that guests always know what comes next without needing instructions. In weddings, this means transitions from one ritual to another feel natural rather than forced. In corporate events, it means sessions, networking and breaks move smoothly without confusion. When flow is respected, guests remain engaged rather than fatigued.

Technology also plays an important role in creating seamless experiences. Reliable sound systems, consistent lighting and stable audiovisual setups ensure that moments are not interrupted. Technical disruptions can quickly break immersion. When technology works quietly in the background, it supports the story rather than distracting from it.

Emotional foresight adds another layer of continuity. Families may need reassurance during emotional moments. Elderly guests may need assistance navigating spaces. Speakers may need guidance before stepping on stage. When these needs are anticipated rather than reacted to, disruptions are minimised. Seamlessness often lies in noticing what others might overlook.

Seamless events are not perfect. Small issues may still occur. What makes them feel seamless is the absence of visible disruption. Challenges are handled quietly. Adjustments are made gently. The experience continues uninterrupted. Guests remember the celebration as a whole rather than as a series of moments.

At its heart, seamlessness is about respect. Respect for time. Respect for emotion. Respect for the guest experience. When an event flows like a well-told story, people remember it the same way. Not in fragments, but as a complete and beautiful memory.

Action Points

- Design transitions carefully: entries, exits, performances, and pauses.
- Keep communication discreet and internal.
- Manage time invisibly so guests never feel rushed.
- Absorb stress internally; never pass it outward.
- Aim for rhythm, not rigidity.

10

How the Right Team Elevates Every Moment

"A great team does not just execute an event. They elevate it."

Behind every memorable celebration stands a team that works quietly, thoughtfully and relentlessly. Weddings, corporate events and social gatherings all rely on people who operate beyond their job descriptions. A strong team does not simply follow instructions. They observe, anticipate and act with ownership. Ek acchi team sirf kaam nahi karti, woh responsibility leti hai.

The right team brings a sense of accountability to every detail. They do not wait to be told what needs attention. They notice when something feels off and step in before it becomes an issue. This proactive mindset transforms execution into care. When teams feel responsible for the experience rather than just the task, quality naturally improves.

Culture plays a defining role in how teams elevate moments. A team that values calmness, respect and empathy behaves differently under pressure. They communicate gently. They support each other. They treat guests with warmth rather than obligation.

Hospitality becomes instinctive rather than scripted. Jab culture sahi hota hai, kaam apne aap better ho jaata hai.

Experience adds another layer of strength. Teams that have handled diverse events develop intuition. They understand crowd behaviour. They anticipate weather challenges. They know vendor dynamics. This experience allows them to respond quickly and confidently when situations change. They do not panic because they have seen complexity before.

The most important quality of the right team is care. Care for the host's vision. Care for the guest experience. Care for the emotions unfolding in the moment. When a team genuinely cares, their work carries heart. Excellence stops being forced and starts feeling natural.

Ultimately, the success of a celebration is not defined by its scale, decor or budget. It is defined by the people who bring it together. The right team elevates moments by creating space for joy, connection and memory. They ensure that when the lights dim and the guests depart, what remains is not exhaustion but fulfilment.

A great team turns moments into memories. And memories are what celebrations are truly about.

Action Points

- Build teams based on attitude and empathy, not just skill.
- Define roles clearly so accountability is shared, not confused.
- Encourage ownership rather than instruction-based working.
- Respect the team; calm teams create calm celebrations.

- Invest in people because great events are built by aligned humans, not checklists.

11

Find Me Here

Instagram

kahani_i2cevents

Instagram

kahani.corporate.events

LinkedIn

Ujjaval Bothra

LinkedIn

kahani-i2cevents

Youtube

@kahani-by-i2cevents

Pinterest

kahanibyi2cevents

Company Website

9 789356 193079

Printed at Repro India Ltd.